W9-AAC-102

David Wright
A Baseball Star Who Cares

Ken Rappoport

Enslow Elementary
an imprint of
Enslow Publishers, Inc.
40 Industrial Road
Box 398
Berkeley Heights, NJ 07922
USA

http://www.enslow.com

E

Enslow Elementary, an imprint of Enslow Publishers, Inc.

Enslow Elementary® is a registered trademark of Enslow Publishers, Inc.

Library of Congress Cataloging-in-Publication Data

Rappoport, Ken.
  David Wright : a baseball star who cares / Ken Rappoport.
      p. cm. — (Sports stars who care)
  Includes bibliographical references and index.
  Summary: "A biography of baseball player David Wright, highlighting his
charitable work"—Provided by publisher.
  ISBN 978-0-7660-3775-5
  1. Wright, David, 1982—Juvenile literature. 2. Baseball players—United States—Biography--
Juvenile literature. 3. Philanthropists—United States—Biography—Juvenile literature. I. Title.
  GV865.W74R37 2011
  796.357092—dc22
  [B]
                                    2010041783

122010 Lake Book Manufacturing, Inc., Melrose Park, IL

Printed in the United States of America

10 9 8 7 6 5 4 3 2 1

To Our Readers:
We have done our best to make sure all Internet addresses in this book were active and
appropriate when we went to press. However, the author and the publisher have no
control over and assume no liability for the material available on those Internet sites or on
other Web sites they may link to. Any comments or suggestions can be sent by e-mail to
comments@enslow.com or to the address on the back cover.

Contents

INTRODUCTION 5

1 Opening Day 7

2 Baseball Lessons 13

3 Drafted by the Mets 20

4 A Clutch Hitter 27

5 Good Times, Bad Times 33

6 A Role Model 40

CAREER STATISTICS
AND WHERE TO WRITE 45

WORDS TO KNOW 46

READ MORE
AND INTERNET ADDRESSES 47

INDEX 48

Introduction

With his friendly smile, David Wright looks and acts like the kid next door. But pitchers have a different view of the New York Mets third baseman. To them, he is a terror. He is one of the most feared hitters in baseball.

In just a few years, Wright has become a star. He hits for power and average. He is a threat to steal bases as well. He signed with the Mets in 2001. Three years later, Wright was in the majors. He was only twenty-one.

He is one of the hardest workers in the game. His many awards include a gold glove as the top third baseman in the National League. Off the field, he has worked hard with charities. His David Wright Foundation helps to make life better for needy children.

"David is so good, on and off the field, that he may well become the face of the franchise," said Jeff Wilpon. Wilpon's family owns the Mets.

Here, then, is the story of Wright's journey from the playing fields of Virginia to the big leagues.

DID YOU KNOW?

In his first seven years in the big leagues, Wright knocked in one hundred or more runs every year he played a full season.

The New York Mets clutch player was in a tough spot. Two runners were on base and his team was losing 5–2. The pressure was on David Wright.

The time: 2009. The event: a star-studded opening of a new ballpark, Citi Field in New York.

Chapter 1

Opening Day

An aerial shot of the new Citi Field a week before it officially opened in 2009.

The opening had created excitement all over town. Also a question: How would the ball carry in the new park?

For just about every season since 1964, the Mets had played in Shea Stadium. Now they were at Citi Field. The new field was larger than the old one.

Would it be harder for players to hit home runs?

No one knew. There was a test.

Citi Field was still under construction in early September 2008. The Mets asked Wright to check out the field.

There were chunks of concrete in the outfield and soil and gravel in the infield. There was no home plate when Wright took batting practice.

He hit a few balls over the wall down the left-field line. Wright and the Mets still were not sure how the ball would carry. The opening day game against the San Diego Padres would tell all.

Game time.

Citi Field opened with Marine jet fighters flying overhead. A sellout crowd filled the stadium. Former Mets star Tom Seaver was on hand to throw the first pitch.

The fans were disappointed when San Diego took the early lead. The Padres led 5–2 when Wright came to bat in the fifth inning.

David Wright takes a big swing—and connects!

Earlier, Wright hit a double. Later he hit a long drive to center field. In the old stadium, it might have been a home run. But the ball was caught in front of the wall of the large new ballpark.

Now it was the fifth inning. Everyone waited to see if Wright could save the day. He stepped into the batter's box with two runners on base. Could he come through for his team?

He got ready for the pitch. Wright swung.

Going, going, gone!

Home run.

As each run came in, the crowd got louder. The fans were out of their seats. They gave Wright a standing ovation as he ran around the bases. Tie score: 5–5.

It was a short-lived joy. The first Mets homer at Citi Field was not enough to provide a victory for the home team. The final score: San Diego 6, New York 5. But Wright had given the fans something to remember. He had hit the first home run for the Mets in the new stadium.

Wright is congratulated at home plate by teammate Carlos Beltran after coming through with a big hit.

"I would have liked to get that win," Wright said. "But it's something I'll look back on, tell my kids, my grandkids, that I was a part of it."

Coming through with big hits was nothing new for Wright. He had been a natural hitter for as far back as anyone could remember.

THWACK! The sound of the bat meeting the ball split the late afternoon air. Then again, the sound. And then again, the sound echoed throughout the neighborhood.

It was a typical spring day. Everywhere, fathers and sons, grandfathers and grandsons, heard the call. Play ball!

Chapter 2

Baseball Lessons

David Wright took his first swings as a young boy with a bat that was given to him by his grandfather.

In the backyard, young David Wright stood holding a wooden bat. He waited for the next pitch. The bat was a present from his granddad. He loved it.

"It was a big, heavy wooden bat," David said.

Bats do not last forever. The bat finally cracked. What did they do?

"After I broke it, it was nailed together. I used it some more," David said.

Growing up in Norfolk, Virginia, David loved baseball. His love of the game started with these fun-filled backyard games with his grandfather. It continued with his father. He was also his Little League coach.

Although he was the son of the coach, David did not expect any favors. In fact, he got none. His father was strict at home. He was just as strict on a baseball field.

"[My parents] didn't set out to raise a good baseball player," David said. "They wanted to raise a good person."

David played for the Green Run Padres. At the age of nine, he was the youngest on the team. He was also one of the best. He loved playing shortstop. One day he came to the field and found that his father had put him in right field. It was a position David hated.

He played, but he was not happy about it.

His father, Rhon, explained: "David was good at short. I told him he had to earn his spot in the field and prove he could make the plays."

His father did it for another reason. He wanted to make sure that David did not think he was more important than his teammates.

"The idea of putting David in right was to instill humility."

David had always been taught by his father to be respectful and kind to others. Usually he was. Sometimes he lost his cool. Playing for another coach, David was taken out of the game for a pinch runner. He was angry. He ripped off his helmet. He slammed it against the ground.

David Wright shares a laugh with a fellow ballplayer outside the batting cage. Wright's love of baseball began with backyard games with his father and grandfather.

"I was scared to death to tell my father," David said. "That was one of the hardest things I've ever had to do, telling my father."

There was another time when David got into trouble. He was eating in the lunchroom when suddenly a French fry hit him in the face. Spotting the kid who threw it, David fired back with a hamburger. Down to the principal's office they went. David got an in-school suspension.

"I read him the riot act," David's father said about the strong lecture he gave his son.

Wright snares a line drive during a play-off game against the St. Louis Cardinals in October 2006.

There were many more good times than bad. David's father was a policeman. One of his assignments took him to the ballpark. The Norfolk Tides were the top farm team of the New York Mets. David tagged along. He became a Tides fan, just like his dad and three brothers.

"I always thought it was the coolest thing" getting autographs, Wright said.

Like every other young fan, David spent time chasing after autographs.

Soon he would be chasing after a dream.

David Wright was getting lots of attention during his teenage years. As the best player on his high school team, offers started to arrive from different colleges. They wanted him to come play for their teams. He was named the Virginia Player of the Year. He joined a

Chapter 3

Drafted by the Mets

David Wright examines his bat during a game. Wright always used wooden bats when he was younger; never metal.

traveling team. His teammates were among some of the best young baseball players in America.

Everyone on the team used a metal bat— except Wright. He insisted on using only wood. Why? He was getting ready for the majors. There are no metal bats in the big leagues.

One day he was waiting to hit in the on-deck circle. He heard a teammate's voice.

"C'mon man, just use metal once."

David shook his head. "I've got to use wood."

Getting annoyed by his teammates' pestering, he finally gave up. He grabbed a metal bat and stalked to home plate.

One swing—home run!

Returning to the dugout, David snapped "There, you happy?"

After that, it was wooden bats all the way.

Before his senior year, he agreed to college baseball for Georgia Tech.

Then the Mets came calling. They had picked David in the first round of the 2001 draft. Third base had been a problem for the Mets. They were hoping Wright would solve the problem.

He and his family had a meeting. He had to decide what to do. Should he finish college or play pro ball? It was a tough decision.

His father was a huge Mets fan. Young David was a big fan of the Mets minor-league team. It would be a dream come true to play for the Mets.

It was not a difficult decision after all. Wright signed with the Mets.

During his early years in the minors, Wright looked like two different players. When he was on the road, his batting average was a puzzle. It was often 100 points higher than when he played at home. What was going on?

Wright Is ready to tag out the runner sliding into third base. Wright worked hard to improve his defense during his rookie year with the Mets.

The Mets finally figured it out. When the team was home, Wright would arrive at practice five hours early to get extra batting practice. By game time he was too tired to be at his best.

Once that problem was solved, Wright moved up quickly through the minor leagues. It was not long before the Mets called him up. Three teams, all in one season! Final stop—the major leagues.

New York, New York. Wright was in the big time. He was only twenty-one when he was placed in the Mets lineup at third base. He continued his power hitting with 14 more home runs.

In 2005, Wright led the Mets with his bat. But his defense needed work. With 24 errors, Wright tied for most errors by a third baseman in the major leagues. He was not happy. He started to put in extra hours on his defense.

"There are so many players out there who are better than me, talent wise," Wright said. "But I like to think I'll outwork all of them."

Wright chases a pop-up into the stands.

The following year, he had cut his errors down to just 19.

Even with all the errors, the 2005 season had a defensive highlight for Wright. It happened when New York was playing against the San Diego Padres.

There was one out in the seventh inning. The Padres batter hit a pop-up about twenty feet beyond the infield dirt.

Wright raced back, turning away from home plate. He stretched out his bare right hand and made a great catch. He tumbled to the grass. He held on to the ball despite his hard fall.

The San Diego fans gave Wright a standing ovation that lasted several minutes.

The play was voted the "This Year in Baseball Play of the Year."

Wright was quickly becoming a superstar.

Batter up, David Wright! All eyes were on the New York Mets third baseman. He stepped to the plate. On the mound, the New York Yankees Mariano Rivera looked in for the sign. It was a big moment in what was known as the

Chapter 4

A Clutch Hitter

David Wright takes swings and comes up with another big hit!

"Subway Series." It was the Mets versus the Yankees.

The score was tied 6–6 in the ninth inning. The Mets had a runner in scoring position at second base. There were two out.

It was a tough spot. Could David Wright come through and bring home the winning run?

Growing up, Wright loved competing against brothers Stephen, Matthew, and Daniel in Ping-Pong, bowling, and video games.

Wright worked the count to 2–2 against the Yankees relief ace. In came the next pitch, a low fastball.

Wright whipped his bat around and made contact. Where would the ball land? He was not sure. He strained to watch the flight of the ball. Excited, Wright ran down the first-base line.

He had smashed the pitch 400 feet to the warning track in center field. It was far over the head of the Yankees center fielder.

In came the winning run. The Mets beat the Yankees, 7–6. Wright's happy teammates rushed to mob him.

It was just another clutch hit by Wright in the 2006 season. By the All-Star break, Wright had knocked in a Mets record 74 runs!

Wright was selected to play in the All-Star Game. He was entered in the Home Run Derby. The night before, Wright had nightmares about getting shut out.

He was afraid he would embarrass himself. The event was on national television. He knew of one famous home-run hitter who had been shut out in the contest. How would he do, he asked himself?

The next day he found out. In the first round, he hit 16 homers. It was the third highest total for any round in Home Run Derby history. The next night, he was batting in his first All-Star Game. What did he do? Facing the American League starter, he slammed a home run.

Wright throws out a
runner at first base.

Back in the regular season, Wright continued his red-hot hitting. The Mets were going to the playoffs. David Wright was leading them. It was their first time in the playoffs since 2000.

His 2006 season earned him a huge raise. The Mets gave Wright a six-year contract extension worth $55 million. Wright was determined to earn every cent.

With fewer errors and a rising batting average, Wright was on his way to reaching his goals.

In his first four full seasons in the major leagues, 2005–2008, the awards and honors piled up for Wright. He was the best hitter and best fielder at his position in the National League.

Two Silver Slugger awards. Two Gold Glove awards. Three All-Star Games.

Could Wright keep up the pace?

The world was watching. It was the 2009 World Baseball Classic. The place: Miami, Florida.

Two outs and the Americans were going home. They were trailing Puerto Rico 5–4 in the bottom of the ninth. David Wright stepped to the plate with the bases loaded.

Chapter 5

Good Times, Bad Times

Wright drives in the winning run as the United States beats Puerto Rico in the World Baseball Classic in 2009.

Chants of "U-S-A", "U-S-A" filled the air.

Wright was ready. He was representing the United States of America. He had to come through. In came a low fastball. Wright smacked it down the right-field line. Two runs scored. The Americans won, 6–5!

DID YOU KNOW?
David's clubhouse nicknames include "Visine" and "Hollywood."

A happy and excited Wright was mobbed by his teammates. Derek Jeter of the New York Yankees was one of the first to reach Wright. The rest of the team followed. It was a wild scene. They piled together, hugging and rolling around on the infield like kids.

The Americans lost in the semifinals. But Wright had stood out in the preseason event featuring the best players in the world. It seemed nothing could stop him. Then something did.

It was August 15, 2009. The Mets were playing a game against the San Francisco Giants.

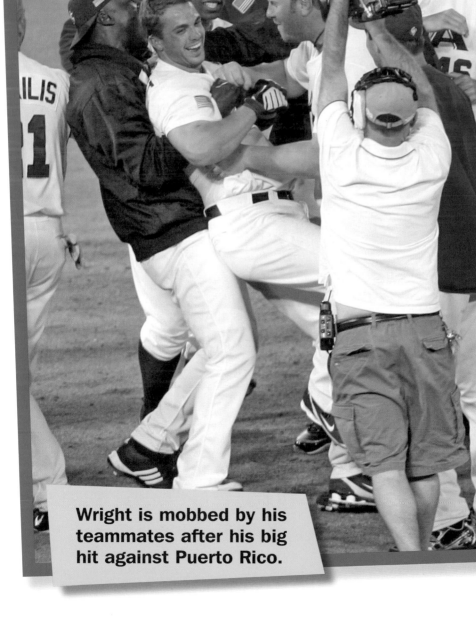

Wright is mobbed by his teammates after his big hit against Puerto Rico.

Wright was up. He stepped in to face the pitcher, Matt Cain. Cain fired a 94-mile-per-hour fastball. It was heading straight for his head. Wright tried to duck. But the pitch hit him on the side of his helmet. His helmet went flying. He dropped to the ground.

DID YOU KNOW?
David Wright was the first Mets player to start his own charity.

A hush fell over Citi Field. Wright lay still, not moving. His face was in the dirt.

Trainers rushed from the dugout to come to Wright's aid. The pitcher moved in closer, fearing what he had done. Several minutes passed.

Finally Wright responded. With help, he got to his feet. He slowly walked off the field with the help of trainers. The crowd cheered.

An ambulance rushed Wright to the hospital. He found out he had suffered a concussion. A concussion is a brain injury caused by a sudden blow. It can make a person feel dizzy or dazed.

David Wright sports a new, bigger batting helmet for extra protection after getting hit by a pitch late in the 2009 season.

Wright suffered from headaches in the days that followed. The Mets put him on the disabled list for fifteen days.

He hated just watching and not being able to help his teammates. He had no choice. He needed an OK from his doctors to return to the game.

Finally he returned to the lineup on September 1 in a game against the Colorado Rockies. Wright was happy to be back on the field. He loves competition. Whether playing cards in the locker room or playing baseball on the field, he hates to lose. He wants to be the best at what he does.

David Wright loves New York. When he was a kid from Virginia, he first thought the city was too big, too scary. Not now.

"I'm more New Yorker than anything," he says. "I feel like I'm

Chapter 6

A Role Model

David Wright and Derek Jeter pose together at a news conference where the two announced a new "batting challenge" to benefit both the David Wright Foundation and Jeter's Turn 2 Foundation.

a part of this town. I drive a little faster now. I talk a little faster."

In 2005, he started his own charity. The David Wright Foundation provides money and support for children's causes, especially research for multiple sclerosis. He is a hero to the children he helps.

"I've always enjoyed helping others less fortunate than myself," Wright said. "I think it's a responsibility in my position to help out. But I have a good time doing it."

The *new* New Yorker has not forgotten his small-town roots in Virginia and what his father told him:

"You're in a position where you can be a positive role model."

Wright enjoys being a role model. Many times there would be long lines of fans at the Mets' games waiting for autographs. Many of the fans were wearing Wright's jersey No. 5.

When he was a kid chasing after autographs, the big stars were usually the hardest to get.

Many times, he walked away from the ballpark disappointed.

He did not want to disappoint the Mets fans. Tired after a game, he stayed. Enjoying his fans, he signed until everyone was happy.

Wright signs autographs while attending the Mets Foundation "Teammates in the Community" fund-raiser.

He is not just popular with the fans. The president of the United States invited him to the White House for dinner along with several other players.

"Oh, man, it was incredible," Wright said. "He [President George W. Bush] didn't take a single call the entire time."

When he is home, Wright likes to play video games to relax. So imagine how excited he was to be on the cover of a popular video game.

Even while enjoying fame, he remembers lessons taught by his father.

"He taught me that it doesn't matter if you're a police officer, a baseball player, or a student. You try to be the best and give 100 percent."

It is the reason Wright has become one of baseball's most exciting and popular players.

Career Statistics

YEAR	TEAM	G	AB	R	H	2B	3B	HR	RBI	SB	AVG
2004	Mets	69	263	41	77	17	1	14	40	6	.293
2005	Mets	160	575	99	176	42	1	27	102	17	.306
2006	Mets	154	582	96	181	40	5	26	116	20	.311
2007	Mets	160	604	113	196	42	1	30	107	34	.325
2008	Mets	160	626	115	189	42	2	33	124	15	.302
2009	Mets	144	535	88	164	39	3	10	72	27	.307
2010	Mets	157	587	87	166	36	3	29	103	19	.283
	TOTALS	1,004	3,772	639	1,149	258	16	169	664	138	.305

G=Games   R=Runs   2B=Doubles   HR=Home runs   SB=Stolen bases
AB=At bats   H=Hits   3B=Triples   RBI=Runs batted in   AVG=Batting Average

Where to Write

MR. DAVID WRIGHT
C/O THE NEW YORK METS
Citi Field
123-01 Roosevelt Avenue
Flushing, NY 11368

All-Star Game—The midseason classic matches the best players in the National and American leagues. Fans get to vote for the starting lineup.

draft—Each year major-league teams select players to fill out their rosters and farm systems. Most of these players are from the amateur ranks.

farm system—All the minor-league teams that are owned by the major-league clubs. There are also other leagues where teams operate independently of the majors.

Gold Glove—The award given to the best defensive player at his position.

major leagues—The American and National leagues make up professional baseball's top two leagues.

minor leagues—All the professional leagues below the major leagues. Class AAA is the highest minor league.

Silver Slugger—The award given to the best offensive player at his position.

third baseman—The position known as the "hot corner." A third baseman must have quick hands and a strong throwing arm.

World Baseball Classic—A tournament featuring the best baseball players from countries around the world.

Read More

Books

Gitlin, Marty. *David Wright: Gifted and Giving Baseball Star*. Berkeley Heights, N.J.: Enslow Publishers, Inc., 2010.

Ross, Alan. *Mets Pride: For the Love of Mookie, Mike and David Wright.* Nashville, Tenn.: Cumberland House Publishing, 2007.

Internet Addresses

David Wright Foundation
http://www.davidwrightfoundation.com

David Wright Official Site
http://www.mlb.com/players/david_wright/index.jsp

New York Mets Official Site
http://newyork.mets.mlb.com

Index

A
All-Star Games, 30, 32
autographs, 19, 42–43
awards, honors, 5, 20, 26, 32, 44

B
bats
    metal *vs.* wood, 21–22
    present of, 15
batting practice, 24

C
Cain, Matt, 37
charity work, 5, 42–43
Citi Field, 7–11
Colorado Rockies, 38
concussion, 37–39

D
David Wright Foundation, 5, 42

G
Georgia Tech, 22
Gold Glove awards, 32
Green Run Padres, 16

H
Home Run Derby, 30
home runs (power hitting), 7–11, 24, 30

J
Jeter, Derek, 35

N
New York Mets
    drafting of David by, 5, 22–24
    farm team of, 19
    New York Yankees *vs.,* 27–30
New York Yankees, 27–30
Norfolk Tides, 19

R
Rivera, Mariano, 27

S
San Diego Padres, 9–12, 26
San Francisco Giants, 35–37
Seaver, Tom, 9
Shea Stadium, 8
Silver Slugger award, 32

T
This Year in Baseball Play of the Year, 26

V
Virginia Player of the Year, 20

W
White House dinner, 44
Wilpon, Jeff, 6
World Baseball Classic 2009, 33–35
Wright, David
    childhood, family life, 15–19
    college, 22
    compensation, 32
    defense, errors, 24–26
    minor league ball, 20–24
    as role model, 42
    work ethic, 5, 26, 32, 39, 44
Wright, Rhon, 15–19

10/12